AN
EASY-READ
FACT
BOOK

Trees

Martyn Hamer

Franklin Watts

London   New York   Toronto   Sydney

© 1983 Franklin Watts Ltd

First published in Great Britain
   1983 by
Franklin Watts Ltd
12a Golden Square
London W1

First published in the USA by
Franklin Watts Inc.
387 Park Avenue South
New York
N.Y. 10016

UK ISBN: 0 86313 015 1
US ISBN: 0-531-04513-7
Library of Congress Catalog Card
   Number: 82-51003

Photographs supplied by
David Jefferis
Frank W. Lane

Illustrated by
James Dugdale
Eagle Artists
Hayward Art Group
Michael Roffe
David Salayia

Designed and produced by
David Jefferis

Technical consultant
Alan Mitchell BA, B.Agric. (For.)

Printed in Great Britain by
   Cambus Litho, East Kilbride

AN
EASY-READ
FACT
BOOK

Trees

Contents

A world of trees

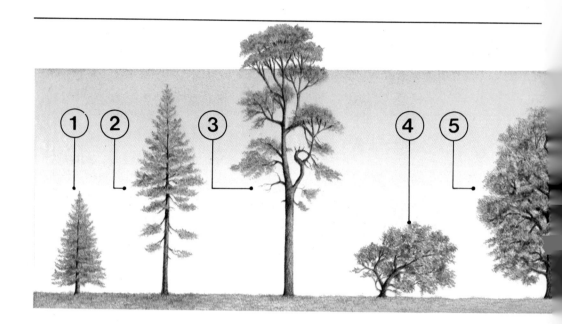

△ The size and shape of trees depend on how old they are and where they grow.
1 Young Scotch pine.
2 Growing up.
3 Mature tree.
4 Oak growing in bare, windy place.
5 Oak growing by itself in a meadow.
6 Forest oak, growing taller to reach the light.

Trees grow in most parts of the world. They can live in many different sorts of surroundings. Some do well in dry areas, others thrive in very damp places. Some grow in flat, low-lying regions, others can be found high up on hillsides.

Deserts, extremely cold places, such as the Arctic and Antarctic, and very high mountain peaks are the only places in the world where trees do not grow.

▷ These Coast Redwoods grow in California, USA. One is the tallest tree in the world at 362 ft (110.3 m).

6

▽ This tiny Sitka spruce took 98 years to grow 11 in (28 cm) tall. It just managed to survive the bitter cold of the Arctic.

The parts of a tree

Plants grow from seeds. They have leaves and usually also have flowers. The main difference between trees and other plants is that trees are bigger and have thick, woody trunks.

A large part of a tree grows under the ground. Here are the roots, which take up water from the soil. In very dry areas trees may have more growth underground than above, so that they can take in as much water as possible. But in most trees the roots spread out roughly as far as, or a little further than the branches.

Water and minerals are taken up the trunk to the upper part of the tree. This is called the crown. The shape of the crown and the way in which the branches grow can vary widely. Some trees, such as the oak, are round and spreading. The branches of a weeping willow hang downwards, but those of the Lombardy poplar slope upwards.

▷ Here you see a broadleaved tree, with its various parts named.

The two main tree groups are broadleaved trees and conifers. Most northern broadleaved trees are deciduous. They drop their flat leaves in autumn and grow new ones in spring. Most conifers are evergreen. They keep their needle-like leaves through the winter.

Broadleaved trees have seeds which are found inside fruits, nuts, pods or berries. The fruits of a conifer are usually cones.

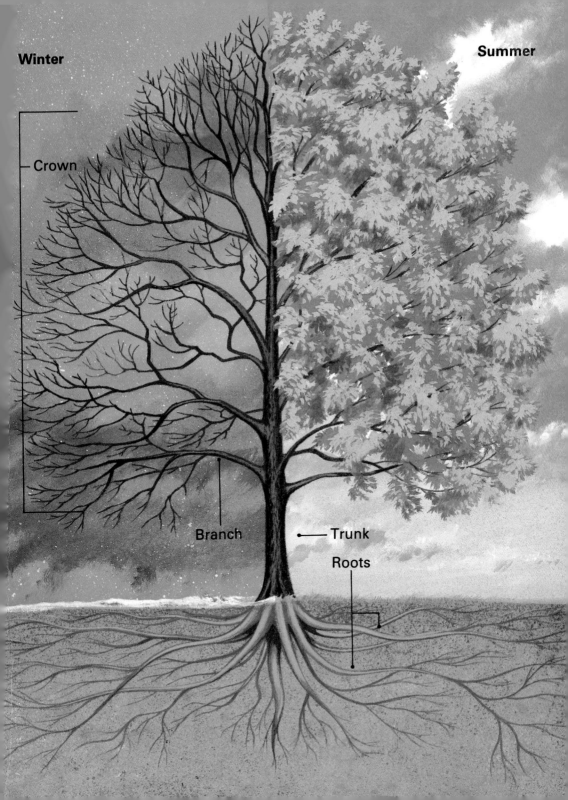

Winter

Summer

Crown

Branch

Trunk

Roots

A look inside the trunk

The outer layer of a tree trunk is the bark. This tough "skin" protects the tree from the weather and creatures that might attack it. Just inside the bark is a thin layer called the phloem. This carries food from the leaves down to the branches, trunk and roots.

Inside the phloem is the layer of cambium. This is the part of the trunk that forms new growth.

Most of the tree trunk is sapwood. It is made up of tubes that carry sap (water and minerals) from the roots to the leaves. The inner core of the tree is called the heartwood. This is dead and solid sapwood that gives the tree its strength.

Sapwood and heartwood together are called the xylem. Running across the xylem are small tubes. These are the medullary rays which carry water and minerals across the trunk and store them.

▷ This diagram shows the different layers in a tree trunk. All new growth is formed by the cambium. When a tree is cut down, this growth shows up as rings of light and dark wood. Each pair of rings represents a year in the life of the tree.

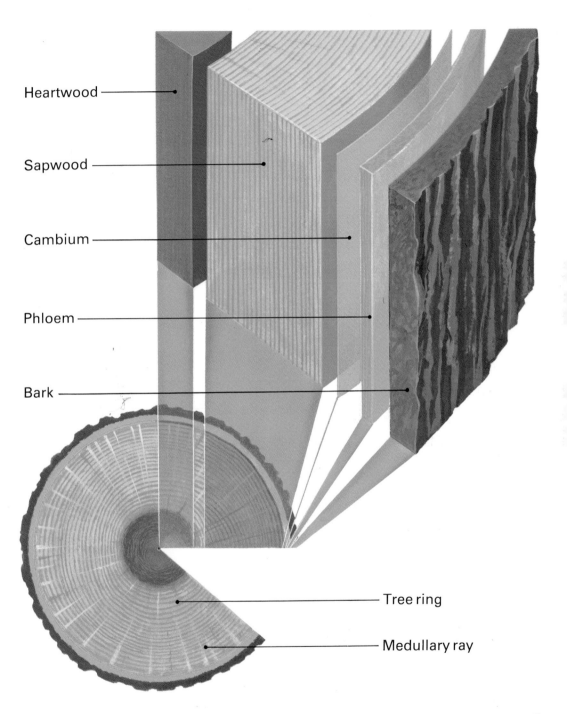

Heartwood

Sapwood

Cambium

Phloem

Bark

Tree ring

Medullary ray

9

Roots and branches

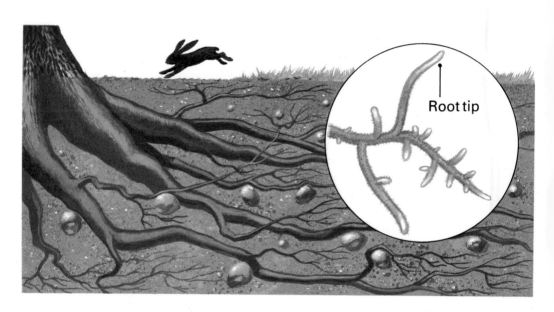

Root tip

△ This picture shows the way that roots spread out beneath the ground. They take in as much water and minerals as they can through the fine hairs on each root tip.

The main task of the roots is to take in water from the soil. This water contains minerals that will help the tree to grow. On a warm day a large tree can take in as much as 260 gallons (1,000 liters) of water.

The tips of the roots are covered with tiny hairs. It is these hairs that collect the water from the soil.

Roots also anchor the tree in the ground and help to hold it upright.

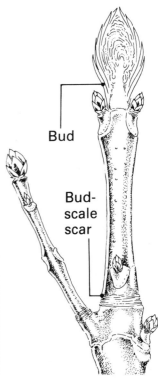

Bud

Bud-
scale
scar

A branch grows longer each year. At the tip of each twig is a bud and from this a new shoot and leaves will sprout. When the growing season is over, new buds form on each twig ready for the next year.

There are several buds on a twig but the leading bud, at the tip, grows the most. If the leading bud is damaged, the next bud down the shoot will usually become the leader.

△ Bud-scale scars are left by the bud when a new shoot forms. You can see how much the twig has grown each year. It is the distance between two scars, or between the last scar and the bud.

The picture on the left shows the branch system of a tree after its leaves have fallen in the autumn.

Leaves

Deciduous leaves

Copper beech (simple)

Horse chestnut
(compound)

Oak (lobed)

Sycamore
(deeply lobed)

△ These are some of the different types of leaves to be found on trees.

Leaves can be all sorts of shapes and sizes. Many conifer leaves are needle-shaped, while broadleaved trees can have either simple or compound leaves. A simple leaf is in one complete piece. Its edge may be smooth or jagged with deep lobes. Compound leaves are made up of three or more separate leaflets.

Coniferous leaves

Sitka spruce

Chile pine or monkey puzzle

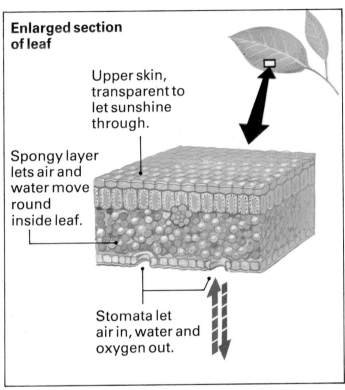

Enlarged section of leaf

Upper skin, transparent to let sunshine through.

Spongy layer lets air and water move round inside leaf.

Stomata let air in, water and oxygen out.

Leaves contain chlorophyll, a green substance that changes sunlight into energy. The tree uses this energy to take in carbon dioxide from the air. The carbon dioxide mixes with water and minerals from the soil to make food — sugar, starch and cellulose. The name for this food–making process is photosynthesis.

△ This picture shows a cross-section through a leaf. The top is tough and usually shiny, to stop the Sun from drying out the leaf. The underside is often hairy. It has tiny openings called stomata. Through these the leaf takes in air and sends out oxygen.

13

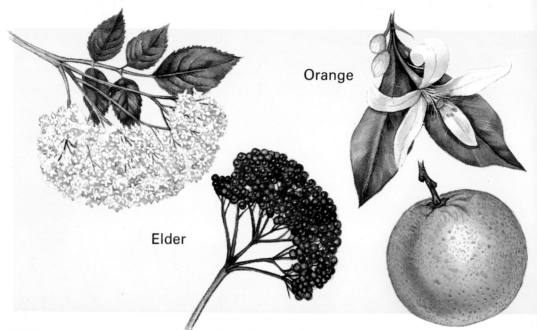

Orange

Elder

Flowers and fruit

Apart from conifers, which produce cones, all trees have flowers. Some are so small and plain that it is hard to spot them. The flowers of the oak and ash are very dull, but trees such as the cherry and apple have bright and attractive blossom.

The flower's task is to produce fruit for the tree. All trees have fruits and these contain the seeds that may one day grow into new trees.

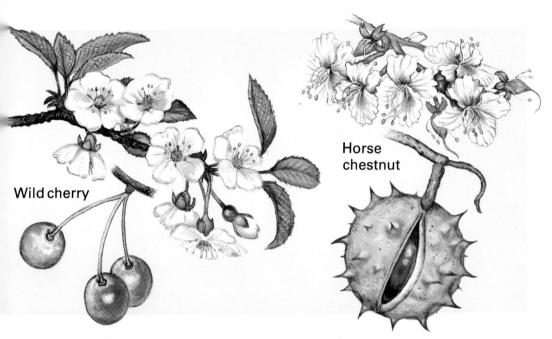

Wild cherry

Horse
chestnut

△ These pictures show
just some of the flowers
and fruits that grow on
trees.

◁ These are the berries
of a five-year-old
mountain ash. Birds love
to eat them.

15

Sowing the seed

△ Every apple core has several pits. These are its seeds. On page 31 you can find out how to grow a tree from a seed.

Even the largest tree grows from a seed, but it takes several years for a young tree to produce seeds of its own. This seed-bearing age is different for each type of tree.

Seeds are spread away from the parent tree by several methods.

Those of the ash and sycamore bear "wings" which can be caught up and carried away by the wind.

Water is another way for seeds to travel. Rain often washes the seeds away from the parent tree. Some seeds are specially adapted for this form of travel and have air sacs to keep them afloat as they drift along.

Many seeds are found inside fruits, nuts, pods or berries. Animals and birds may carry them away to eat but may drop them, or store and then forget them. Even if the fruit is eaten, the seeds are usually left behind and may then grow into trees.

△ These seeds are scattered by the wind. Many seeds have a kind of "wing" to fly through the air for long distances.

◁ Squirrels like acorns and other nuts. They store them away as food for winter, but sometimes forget where they have hidden them. Some of the acorns may grow into trees.

Seedlings

All through the winter a seed lies in the soil. With the coming of spring it begins to grow. First a root grows down into the soil, to take up the water and minerals the plant needs for growth.

When the root is firmly bedded, the seed produces a shoot. This shoot

▽ The picture below shows the early stages of a seed's growth.

pushes up through the soil and into the light. When it gets above ground, it produces two leaves and a bud. These seed leaves are not the same shape as those of a fully grown tree. They contain a store of food which helps the young plant to grow.

In time the bud will open and the first true leaves will form. The two seed leaves will then drop off. As the plant grows, so do the roots, for more water will be needed to help it develop into a mature tree.

▽ Few seeds grow into trees. Many die or are eaten. Those which do grow can still be destroyed. This rabbit has stripped some tasty bark from a sapling. With its phloem destroyed, the tree will die, as no food can go down to the roots.

Life in a tree

A tree makes a home for many insects, birds and other animals. The oak is a good example of a tree home.

On the leaves there may be lots of caterpillars and moths. Many different types of moth which feed on oak leaves have been found in the United States of America.

Perhaps the tree will attract some squirrels. They scamper along the branches looking for the acorns they love to eat.

Ladybirds and other small beetles will often visit oak trees to feed on the small wasps and mites which live in the bark and leaves. Birds also eat many of these small creatures and may build their nests in the tree.

Brown spongy balls can often be seen on oak trees. These are called oak apples, but they are not a fruit. They are caused by the grub of the gall wasp.

▷ These pictures show some of the creatures you could see in or around an oak tree. Other trees may provide a home for many other creatures. Every tree is teeming with life. If you take a close look at any tree you may be surprised at the number of interesting things you will see.

Blackbird

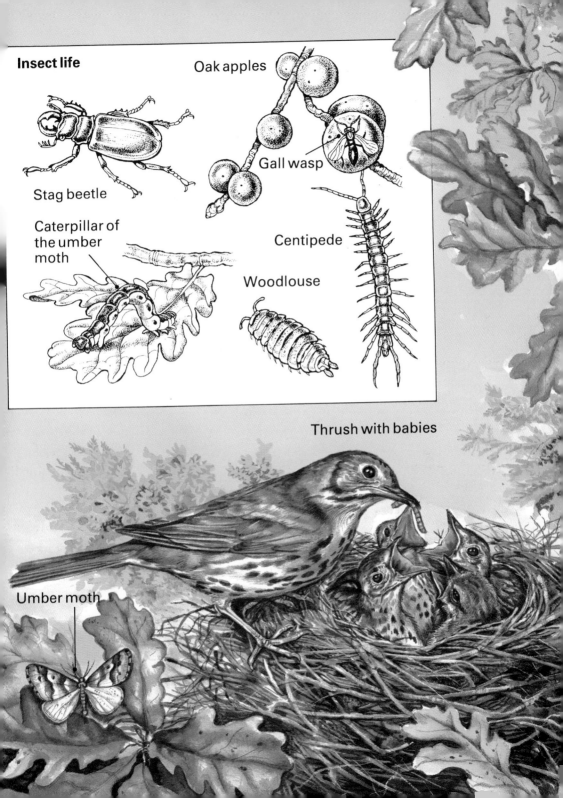

Insect life

Oak apples

Stag beetle

Gall wasp

Caterpillar of
the umber
moth

Centipede

Woodlouse

Thrush with babies

Umber moth

How old is it?

△ This elm remains standing even though it is dead, killed by Dutch elm disease. It will soon be chopped down and cut up for firewood.

The oldest living thing in the world is a tree. Trees can live longer than any other plant or animal.

Some trees grow faster than others but the slow growers usually live longest. A birch tree grows quickly but will rarely live for much more than 60 years. Oak trees and limes grow more slowly, but they can live for about 400 years. A yew tree, which grows very slowly, may live for over 1,000 years.

In America there are bristlecone pines that have lived for almost 5,000 years. They were seedlings when the pyramids of Egypt were being built.

Like other living things, trees die when they grow old. They may also be killed by changes in climate, by fire, disease, or by being chopped down for timber. Much of the forests of South America, for example, are being cleared for farmland.

△ The oldest tree in the world was a bristlecone pine. It was found to be about 4,900 years old when it died. The oldest one still alive is "just" 4,600 years old.

◁ This slowly rotting stump is home to many beetles and other insects.

Forestry

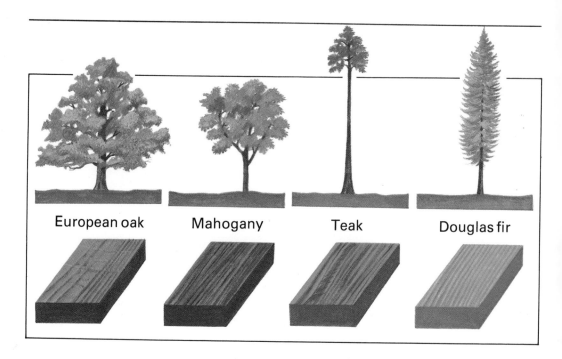

European oak   Mahogany   Teak   Douglas fir

△ Many trees provide wood that can be used in a number of ways. The picture shows some of the most popular woods and the trees from which they come.

It was once thought that there were enough trees to keep the world supplied with timber for ever. Millions of trees were cut down and no one planted new ones to replace them.

It was not until the 20th century that people realised that there could be a serious timber shortage. Today, the cutting down of trees is strictly controlled in many countries.

Much of our timber is grown in large

man-made forests. They are mostly of pine or spruce. Conifers like these grow quickly and have long, straight trunks. This makes them very easy to saw into planks, with little waste. When the trees are felled and taken to the sawmill, the land is cleared and new ones are planted.

In this way, foresters try to ensure there will be a constant supply of wood for the future.

△ A Sitka spruce being chopped down for timber. This huge tree is growing in a suitable climate — compare it with the stunted tree on page 5.

Fire!

"Fire!" This is the cry that foresters most fear, for fire is their worst enemy. When fire rages through the forest, it burns everything in its path.

Once a forest fire starts it is very difficult to put out. Vast areas of forest are destroyed by fire every year. In Canada more than 5,500 sq miles (14,245 sq km) of forest were burned to

▽ One way to fight forest fires is to bomb the burning area with water. Special planes, like this CL-215, can scoop up 1,300 gallons (5,000 liters) of water from a lake and drop it on the flames.

the ground in 1978. This is why many forests have watch-towers manned by forestry officers who look for a first tell-tale wisp of smoke.

As well as destroying trees, fire also kills other plants, insects, birds and animals. After a bad fire it takes many years for the forest to return to normal. It may never recover completely.

If you go for a walk in a forest, remember to follow the forest code. Never leave bottles or broken glass lying about — sunlight shining through glass can start a fire.

The wonder of wood

△ Almost all boats were made of wood until the 20th century. Both this 19th-century lifeboat and the sinking passenger ship are made of wood.

Look around your home and you will see many of the uses of wood. The floor boards, roof supports, doors and window frames may all be made of wood and so may a lot of your furniture. Wood is also used to make paper and cardboard.

There are 20,000 different types of tree in the world, but only about 500 of these are used for lumber. Other trees are grown for the fruit they bear, but

trees provide many other products which are useful to us.

Eucalyptus oil is used in some medicines and comes from the leaves of the eucalyptus tree. Chewing gum is made from the sap of the sapodilla tree. Rubber is made from the latex of the rubber tree. Most cork is the bark of the cork oak, and other barks are used for food flavoring, medicines and for tanning leather.

△ Here are just some of the things you might find in the home that come from trees. Try making a tour around your own home to discover the tree products in it. You will be surprised at the number of them!

Glossary

Tree facts

Here is a list of some of the technical words used in this book.

Here are some interesting and unusual facts about the world of trees.

Broadleaved tree
One of the two main tree groups. These trees have leaves which drop off in autumn.

Cambium
Layer which forms new growth. Phloem is on the outside, sapwood on the inside.

Carbon dioxide
Colorless gas, present in the air.

Chlorophyll
Material which makes plants green. It turns sunlight into chemical energy. This is used to change carbon dioxide, minerals and water into glucose, a plant's food.

Conifer
One of the two main tree groups. Conifers usually keep their leaves through the winter.

Deciduous trees
Trees which drop their leaves in autumn, growing new ones the following spring.

Evergreen trees
Trees that keep their leaves in winter.

Phloem (*FLOW-em*)
Layer that carries food from the leaves to the rest of the tree.

Photosynthesis
Name given to the food-making process in plants.

Sapwood
Layer which carries water and minerals up from the roots to the leaves.

Xylem (*ZY-lem*)
The name given to a tree's inner layers of sapwood and heartwood.

The belly palm
The belly palm grows on the sandy plains of Pinar del Rio in western Cuba. It has an odd-looking bottle-shaped trunk and looks rather like a snake which has just swallowed a large mouse. Its wood is used to make casks, beehives and small boats.

The dynamite tree
This strange tree grows in Mexico. It bears fruits called gourds which are about the size of an orange. These explode when ripe, scattering hard fragments up to 23 ft (7 m) away! Luckily, this rather dangerous tree is quite rare!

A poisonous tree
The "tree of the bad

30

woman" grows in remote parts of the Mexican state of Morelos. If you touch the tree, you will break out with skin rashes and suffer a raging fever. Warning signs are put nearby to keep people away. . . .

The biggest living thing
A Giant Sequoia in California is the biggest living thing on Earth. Its name is General Sherman and experts reckon that five billion matches could be made from it. Its weight is thought to be more than 2,200 tons (2,000 tonnes).

Growing a seedling

With some care and attention, you can grow your own tree from a seed in spring. Any seed will do, acorns or even apple pits. Don't be too impatient – the seeds will take six to eight weeks to sprout.
1 Soak the seeds overnight in water. This is very useful if you are planting nuts such as acorns. Take the "cup" off an acorn.
2 Put small stones in the bottom of a flower pot, then fill it up with fine soil or compost. Water the soil well, then put your seed on top. Cover it with a thin layer of soil, pressing down firmly. Water again, then fasten a clear plastic bag over the pot, using string or a rubber band. Put the pot in a light place.
3 As soon as you see a seedling popping through the soil, take off the bag. Water the seedling every few days, but remember if it gets too wet it may rot. In the summer, you can put the pot outside. Later on, in the autumn, you can plant the seedling in the ground. In a few years you will have a fine young sapling.

31

Index